# ADVERTISING

## GLOBAL CITIZENS: MODERN MEDIA

Published in the United States of America by Cherry Lake Publishing
Ann Arbor, Michigan
www.cherrylakepublishing.com

Content Adviser: Jessica Haag, MA, Communication and Media Studies
Reading Adviser: Cecilia Minden, PhD, Literacy expert and children's author

Photo Credits: ©Elnur/Shutterstock.com, Cover, 1; Photo by Matthewhuested/Public Domain/Wikimedia Commons, 5; George Johann Scharf/Public Domain/Wikimedia Commons, 6; ©mikeyashworth/flickr.com, 7; ©Everett Collection/Shutterstock.com, 8; ©Pixabay/pixabay.com, 10; ©Suzanne Tucker/Shutterstock.com, 13; ©Morrowind/Shutterstock.com, 14; ©ESB Professional/Shutterstock.com, 15; ©nazarovsergey/Shutterstock.com, 16; ©photobyphm/Shutterstock.com, 19; ©Jonathan Weiss/Shutterstock.com, 20; ©ArliftAtoz2205/Shutterstock.com, 21; ©mimohe/Shutterstock.com, 22; ©Shyamalamuralinath/Shutterstock.com, 23; ©ImageFlow/Shutterstock.com, 24; ©wavebreakmedia/Shutterstock.com, 27, 28

Copyright ©2019 by Cherry Lake Publishing
All rights reserved. No part of this book may be reproduced or utilized in
any form or by any means without written permission from the publisher.

Library of Congress Cataloging-in-Publication Data has been filed and is available at catalog.loc.gov

Cherry Lake Publishing would like to acknowledge the work of the Partnership for 21st Century Learning.
Please visit www.p21.org for more information.

Printed in the United States of America
Corporate Graphics

## ABOUT THE AUTHOR

Wil Mara has been an author for over 30 years and has written more than 100 educational titles for children. His books have been translated into more than a dozen languages and won numerous awards. He also sits on the executive committee for the New Jersey affiliate of the United States Library of Congress. You can find out more about Wil and his work at www.wilmara.com.

# TABLE OF CONTENTS

**CHAPTER 1**
## History:
## Advertising Through the Years ........... 4

**CHAPTER 2**
## Geography:
## Advertising Around the World ........... 12

**CHAPTER 3**
## Civics:
## How Advertising Works ...................... 18

**CHAPTER 4**
## Economics:
## The Numbers Behind the Ads ........... 26

THINK ABOUT IT ....................................................... 30
FOR MORE INFORMATION ............................................... 31
GLOSSARY ............................................................. 32
INDEX ................................................................ 32

# CHAPTER 1

# History: Advertising Through the Years

People have been communicating with each other for thousands of years. What began as rock carvings has slowly changed into books, newspapers, magazines, movies, radio, TV, and the Internet. Together, they are called **media**.

**Advertising** is a way for businesses to communicate to many people using different types of media. The **commercials** you watch on television, hear on the radio, or see online are there because some company created a **product**, service, or idea that they want to sell.

## In Early Times

There is evidence of advertising starting thousands of years ago. Archaeologists uncovered signs and wall paintings for

H.S. Tyler creatively advertised his run for mayor in 1893.

businesses, like hotels, bars, and restaurants, in Pompeii. This ancient city was buried by a volcanic eruption in 79 CE. One of the earliest discovered printed advertisements, or ads, comes from China during the Song dynasty (960–1279 CE). It was a simple ad for sewing needles that read: "We buy high quality steel rods and make quality fine needles, to be ready for use at home in no time."

Advertising took a leap forward following Johannes Gutenberg's invention of the **printing press** in the mid-1400s. Where it used to take hours to create ads by hand, a press could turn out hundreds at a time. Before Gutenberg's press was invented, the

*People in the past and still today carry around billboards to advertise a product or service.*

majority of advertising was done by **word of mouth**, or recommendations from workers or customers. The printing press revolutionized not only advertising but also communication in general.

## Broadcast Media

The majority of ads were published in print media, like newspapers and magazines, until the rise of the radio in the 1920s. At first, the radio was used only to communicate news and other important announcements. No one wanted advertising to be a

Since as early as the 15th century, people would legally and illegally stick advertising posters on buildings.

Before TV and the Internet, people would look forward to shows on the radio.

part of it. Even the first ads on the radio were considered a public service effort. In 1922, a real estate company ran a 10-minute commercial advertising apartments. After its success, more and more companies started to buy radio ad space.

Radio ushered in a new kind of media: **broadcast**. Not long after that came television. Television started popping up in homes around the 1940s and 1950s. The first commercial advertised Bulova, a high-end watch and jewelry company. It was only a 10-second commercial and seen by only a few thousand people.

But it radically changed advertising and propelled it forward. By the 1990s, the average hour-long television program, or TV show, had almost 20 minutes of commercials!

## Digital Advertising

Before Google Chrome, Mozilla Firefox, and even Internet Explorer, there was Netscape. Netscape was a browser that helped the average Internet user go online. Companies were determined to figure out a way to promote their business in this new space. In 1994, AT&T was the first to run an online ad. Forty-four percent of the people who saw the **banner ad** actually clicked on it. The average **click through rate** for a banner ad today is less than 1 percent globally. This big difference might be because

### Pictures Instead of Words

*During the Middle Ages, European businessmen were faced with the challenge of advertising to people who couldn't read. They got around this problem by putting pictures on their signs instead of words. For example, a picture of a bed might be used to advertise a hotel.*

As of April 2017, Facebook had an estimated 5 million advertisers on its social media platform.

10

in 1994 there was only one type of online ad. It was also a new concept. People were curious. Today, there are countless ways companies advertise online, from pop-up ads to video ads. Ads are something we see every day.

Advertisers are now taking advantage of social media, a new source of digital media. Social advertising, or advertising using social media, has grown in a short period of time. In 2014, $16 billion was invested in social media advertising worldwide. Two years later, this number was $31 billion, almost double. Advertisers prefer Internet-based advertising, like social media. That's because for the first time ever, they can accurately track who, when, and where the **audience** is clicking.

## Developing Questions

*Advertisers are getting better at focusing on individual people rather than on groups. It has reached the point where someone will see online ads based on previous purchases. What benefits do you see coming from this? What problems might come from it?*

# CHAPTER 2

# Geography: Advertising Around the World

There are advertising laws all around the world. These laws are designed to protect **consumers**. Those are the people who buy a company's product or service.

## United States

The average child in the United States will see at least 20,000 commercials over the course of 1 year. That child will have seen about 6 million commercials by the age of 16. This happens even though the Children's Television Act (CTA) of 1990 limits the amount of ads broadcast during children's television shows.

Studies show that children as young as 2 years old recognize and prefer one brand over another. This might be due to the increase in advertising.

Commercials aren't the only way advertisers promote a product. In fact, it's not even the most popular. As of 2016, digital advertising, or ads online, made $1.2 billion more than television ads in the

## Watchdog Agencies

*The Australian Competition and Consumer Commission keeps watch on all advertising in that country. It acts as an "advertising police force" for consumers who feel they've been misled. The United States' version of this agency is known as the Federal Trade Commission (FTC).*

[ Advertising ]

According to the American Psychological Association (APA), children under 8 believe everything they see and hear.

United States. Because of the evolving nature of the Internet, the government passed the Children's Online Privacy Protection Act (COPPA) in 2000. It protects users under 13 years old. Despite the CTA and COPPA, the United States does far less to regulate the ad industry than many other countries.

The number of advertising and marketing jobs in the United Kingdom increased by 33 percent between 2011 and 2016.

In New Zealand, more than one in eight children are obese. Many believe this is because of the increase in junk food advertising.

## Norway

In 2004, food and beverage companies in Europe were instructed by the European health commissioner to stop advertising to children. Norway already had strict laws and regulations surrounding advertising. The country's Broadcasting Act of 1992 said advertisers were not allowed to target anyone under the age of 12. In 2013, that country's food industry agreed to ban all advertisement of unhealthy foods and drinks to people under 16 years old.

## Cuba

There are a few countries where little to no advertising is present. Cuba is one of them. In most countries, businesses compete with other businesses. The opposite is true for Cuba. Because the government provides everything from food to education to health care, there is little competition. Without competition, there isn't a need for ads. You could walk down a street in Cuba and see virtually no posters or billboards!

### Gathering and Evaluating Sources

*Many countries are starting to limit and even ban junk-food advertising to kids as old as 18! Using the Internet and your local library, gather information about the different countries that ban the promotion of junk food. Which countries have fewer regulations? Which have stricter laws? Why might countries want companies to stop advertising junk food to kids? Use the information you find to support your answer.*

## CHAPTER 3

# Civics: How Advertising Works

The main purpose of advertising is to leave a lasting impression. A company's goal is to plant a strong suggestion about the product that's for sale. There are a few classic ways advertisers will do this.

### Repetition and Slogans

Do you know the company that uses the **slogan** "Just Do It"? What about "Taste the Rainbow"? If you guessed Nike and Skittles, then you're right! One of the most effective ways to get someone thinking about a product is to tell them about it over and over. This is called **effective frequency**. Nike has been repeating its slogan since 1988. Skittles has been repeating its slogan since 1994.

The clothing company Gap briefly changed its logo in 2010. It immediately changed it back after a week because its customers didn't like it.

In 2016, Comcast spent about $5.62 billion on ads.

The best advertisers will use a catchy slogan and repeat it. Studies have shown that statements appear truer the more times they are repeated. If you hear about the same product 10 times in a day, it's going to stick in your brain. Plus you're likely to trust that brand over the others. The next time you need shoes or want candy, Nike and Skittles might just be the first brands to pop into your head.

Many companies use cars to advertise their product or service.

Publicity stunts also help advertise companies and their products.

Many watch brands set their watches to 10:10 because it looks like a smiley face.

## Positive Association

When advertisers connect their product with something or someone people already like, they are using **positive association**. If a company is selling footballs, the ad might feature a famous football player. Advertisers want people to associate their product with the good feelings they have for the celebrity. They're hoping this will help with sales.

Another approach is to connect a product with a certain lifestyle. This is called **lifestyle branding**. Companies want

Studies found that colors can play a significant role in an advertisement.

you to feel like you'll live the lifestyle they're selling if you buy their product. Drink brands, like Coca-Cola, "sell" happiness. Their ads almost always feature friends hanging out and having fun. Athletic labels, like Nike and lululemon, want you to feel like you're leading a healthier life.

## Using Numbers

Some advertisers will point out a fact about their product and hope that consumers will be impressed enough to buy it. Many toothpastes advertise that they are the "number 1 recommended [toothpaste] by dentists." Lysol advertises that its cleaning products "kill 99.9 percent of germs." Adding these facts and statistics help their products stand out and appear more trustworthy.

## Developing Claims and Using Evidence

The term **false advertising** refers to any type of ad that either **exaggerates** facts or lies in order to sell products. In the United States, nearly 5.4 million consumers were awarded more than $160 million as a result of action taken against advertisers for false or misleading claims. In 2016, the FTC sued Volkswagen for false advertising. Volkswagen advertised that it had eco-friendly cars. It turns out they had been cheating on tests for 7 years!

Ads make claims all the time. But that doesn't mean you should accept them as fact. The key is to locate as much information and evidence about the claim as possible. One good idea would be to read reviews from other customers. Think of an ad you just saw. What is the company claiming? Can you find evidence for and against the claim?

# CHAPTER 4

# Economics: The Numbers Behind the Ads

Advertising isn't just a way to help businesses make more money. It's a massive business itself. Some companies handle their own advertising. Others hire ad agencies that keep up with all the changes happening in the fast-growing world of digital advertising.

## A Billion-Dollar Industry

Over the last 5 years, spending on advertising grew at a rate of almost 5 percent each year. In 2017 alone, more than $500 billion was spent globally on advertising. The United States is the leading market in advertising. It spent an estimated $200 billion—almost

The American Advertising Federation (AAF) was founded in 1905. AAF helps people further their advertising careers.

half of the global spending! China, the second-largest market, only spent a little more than $80 billion.

Around $100 billion was spent on print media, like magazines and newspapers. Another $100 billion went to broadcast advertising, like television and radio commercials. The largest amount spent went to digital advertising.

## Digital Advertising

For the first time, digital advertising beat television in ad spending in 2016. Globally, advertisers spent more than $200 billion

The average 30-second commercial shown during the 2017 Super Bowl cost more than $5 million.

in digital ads. This means digital advertising is about 41 percent of the ad market! It's no wonder digital advertising is appealing.

## Taking Informed Action

*Most companies don't run dishonest ads, but this doesn't mean they don't try to stretch the truth or appeal to your emotions. The next time you see an ad, try to spot the different ways the advertiser is trying to sell the product to you. Are they selling you the product or a lifestyle or feeling? Chapter 3 and other sources online can help you identify the different techniques advertisers use to get you to buy. Share the information you find with your friends and family.*

In traditional print media, a typical full-page ad in a magazine can run as much as $221,000. Digital advertising, on the other hand, is flexible. A company can spend as little as a few dollars to promote something on social media, like Twitter, Facebook, or Instagram. Even more attractive is that they can tailor different ads to be seen by different **demographics**.

## Traditional Print Media

The traditional printed ad is still important—at least for now. One study reported that 58 percent of **subscribers** say they prefer physical newspapers and magazines over digital copies. But it's important to note the age difference. The majority of the people who preferred physical copies were far older than those who preferred digital copies. This means that 58-percent figure is likely to gradually decrease over the years.

### Communicating Conclusions

*Before reading this book, did you know about advertising? Now that you know more, why do you think it's important to know about the industry and the tactics advertisers use? Based on what you've read and the research you've done, what do you think advertisers will do next? What approaches and techniques—no matter how crazy they might sound—do you think they might try?*

[ ADVERTISING ]

# Think About It

**Augmented reality** (AR) is one of the new growing trends in digital advertising. It's a technique that places a computer-generated image into real life using a mobile device. Pokémon GO is an example of AR technology. But it's not just about games. Businesses are now using AR as a way to advertise. In 2013, IKEA used AR to promote its 2014 furniture lineup. Users were able to "place" furniture in their homes. In 2014, businesses worldwide spent $600 million in AR ad spending. This number has skyrocketed to $12.8 billion in 2017.

In 2016, data showed that the average American adult viewed 10 hours and 39 minutes of digital media every day. Keep in mind the average American adult is only awake for 17.2 hours a day. What does this tell you about consumers? Also, what do you think this means for the traditional forms of advertising, like ads in newspapers and magazines or television and radio commercials? How do you think the world of media is likely to change in the future?

# For More Information

## Further Reading

Minden, Cecilia. *Starting Your Own Business*. Ann Arbor, MI: Cherry Lake Publishing, 2016.

Perdew, Laura. *Asking Questions About Food Advertising*. Ann Arbor, MI: Cherry Lake Publishing, 2015.

Thomson, Ruth. *The Power of Advertising: How Adverts Have You Hooked*. New York: Hachette Children's Group, 2017.

## Websites

**Federal Trade Commission—Admongo**
https://www.consumer.ftc.gov/admongo
Learn about how ads work through this fun, interactive game.

**Federal Trade Commission—You Are Here**
https://www.consumer.ftc.gov/sites/www.consumer.ftc.gov/files/games/off-site/youarehere/index.html
At this virtual mall, you can learn how to be a smarter shopper and even design your own ad!

# GLOSSARY

**advertising** (AD-ver-tize-ing) the practice of telling people about a product in hopes of selling as many or as much as possible

**audience** (AW-dee-ens) a group of people with a common interest

**augmented reality** (awg-MENT-ed ree-AL-ih-tee) an enhanced version of reality created by the use of technology to overlay digital information on an image of something being viewed through a device, like a smartphone

**banner ad** (BAN-ur AD) an advertisement across the top, bottom, or side of a webpage

**broadcast** (BRAWD-kast) transmission of a program or information, as it relates to television and radio

**click through rate** (KLIK THROO RAYT) the percentage of people visiting a webpage from clicking on an advertisement

**commercials** (kuh-MUR-shuhlz) types of advertisement that usually involves some type of video or audio element (or both)

**consumers** (kun-SOO-merz) people who buy things with the intent of using (consuming) them

**demographics** (dem-uh-GRAF-iks) the qualities, like age, sex, and income, of a specific group of people

**effective frequency** (i-FEK-tiv FREE-kwun-see) the number of times a person sees an advertisement before responding

**exaggerates** (ig-ZAJ-uh-rates) makes something seem bigger, better, more important, or more extreme than it really is

**false advertising** (FAWLS AD-ver-tize-ing) the use of false or unproven information to advertise a product or service

**lifestyle branding** (LAHYF-stahyl BRAND-ing) marketing a certain lifestyle in order to sell a service or product

**media** (ME-dee-uh) a method of communication between people, such as a newspaper

**positive association** (POZ-i-tiv uh-soh-see-EY-shuhn) using people's feelings about something or someone, like a famous athlete, and associating it with something else, like a product a company is selling

**printing press** (PRINT-ing PRESS) a device designed to print ink onto paper in large quantities

**product** (PRAH-dukt) an item intended for sale

**slogan** (SLOH-guhn) a phrase or motto used by a business, a group, or an individual to express a goal or belief

**subscribers** (suhb-SKRIBE-erz) people who pay money regularly for a product or service, such as a newspaper or magazine

**word of mouth** (WURD UV MOUTH) the practice of talking to other people about a certain product

# INDEX

advertising, 4, 6, 7, 8, 9, 11–13, 15–18, 25, 26, 27–30
   digital advertising, 9, 13, 26, 27–29, 30
   early times, 4, 5, 6, 7
   false advertising, 25
   laws, 12, 16, 17

billboards, 6, 17

Children's Television Act, 12, 14

commercials, 4, 8, 9, 12, 13, 27, 28, 30

consumers, 12, 13, 24, 25, 30

demographics, 29

junk food, 16, 17

printing press, 5, 6

product, 4, 6, 12, 13, 18, 20–25, 28

slogan, 18, 20

social media, 10, 11, 29